CLASSIC COOKING
Family favourites made with love

Cheree Heath

To Thelma-Polly-Mum-Nana-Granny
With love forever x
- Cheree

Copyright © 2019

All rights reserved. No part of this publication may be reproduced, stored in a retrieval system or transmitted in any form by any means without the prior permission of the copyright owner. Enquiries should be made to the publisher.

Every effort has been made to ensure that this book is free from error or omissions. However, the Publisher, the Author, the Editor or their respective employees or agents, shall not accept responsibility for injury, loss or damage occasioned to any person acting or refraining from action as a result of material in this book whether or not such injury, loss or damage is in any way due to any negligent act or omission, breach of duty or default on the part of the Publisher, the Author, the Editor, or their respective employees or agents.

The Author, the Publisher, the Editor and their respective employees or agents do not accept any responsibility for the actions of any person - actions which are related in any way to information containted in this book.

The moral right of the author has been asserted.

National Library of Australia Cataloguing-in-Publication entry

Author: Heath, Cheree (HH Dip FN & DEA)

Title: Classic Cooking - Family favourites made with love

ISBN: 9781925900989

Subject: Cooking, Food, Recipes

Dewey Number: 641.5

Images by agreement with photographers. Illustrations by Eva Katerina. The publisher has done its utmost to attribute the copyright holders of all the visual material used. If you nevertheless think that a copyright has been infringed, please contact the publisher.

Published by: Fiosracht Press (An import of Of The World Publishing)
ACN 133 333 141
PO Box 8070
Bendigo South LPO VIC 3550

www.oftheworldbooks.com

Contents

6 — remember when...
simple cooking and recipes handed down over the generations

8 — back in the day
how did we eat before things got so complicated!

10 — grow your own
one of the easiest ways to ensure your food is good

12 — basics
stocking a pantry
pastry
butters

24 — soups & starters
pea & ham soup
lamb & vege soup
chicken broth
savoury scones
bacon scone roll
bubble & squeak
cold meat fritters

40 — sauces
mayonnaise
aioli
tartare sauce
seafood sauce
mushroom sauce
pepper sauce
mustard
red wine sauce

58 — mains
cornish pasty
steak & kidney pie
chicken mushroom pie
egg & bacon pie
cheese & tomato flan
roast pork
silverside
baked stuffed topside
carpet bag steak
beef burgundy
herbed rack of lamb
veal cordon bleu
tuna rice slice
farmers chicken casserole
baked lamb chops

90 — vegetables
scalloped potatoes
stuffed mushrooms
baked tomato
baked carrots
parsnip croquettes
baked avocado
cauliflower au gratin
buttered cucumbers

108 — desserts
apple crumble
lemon meringue pie
chocolate mousse
jam roly poly
treacle pudding
chocolate pudding
golden syrup dumplings
apple pie
pavlova roll
brandy snaps
cream puffs
rhubarb apple sponge
lemon cheesecake

136 — dieting
The crazy (and sometimes smart) ways we used to watch the waistline

139 — index & notes
space to record your own family favourites and an easy-to-find ingredient & recipe list

Remember when...

I have always loved to cook. Growing up, my mother and grandmother were a great influence on my appreciation of good food and cooking. My grandmother, who we called Granny, was from the Lakes District in England. She loved to work in the garden, sew and make delicious food. It was a huge shock when she moved to Australia at 18 and, unable to cope with Australia's heat, had to cut up her beautifully embroidered linen to make new clothes for herself.

As a child, I would spend my school holidays with Granny and I remember that Monday was a special baking day. She would cook cakes or sponges, slices or biscuits and make pastries and pies for the week. She would plan all her meals and I can recall her kitchen in great detail: old scales with weights, spoons and cups of all different sizes for measuring, a huge sieve with a handle to sift dry ingredients and everything was cooking in a wooden stove without any temperature controls. It was a magical place and the results were always delicious.

In Granny's era, processed food didn't exist. Food was cooked from scratch and leftovers were used for another meal. People weren't aware of low fat, low sugar or low calories. You followed recipes that had been handed down from your mother and grandmother and making them and sharing them with your loved ones was part of the joy of cooking. A good, balanced diet was the norm (if you were lucky enough to afford it!) and meals were presented on a dinner plate that was far smaller than those we eat off today.

Cooking is still a family affair for me - my mother passed away not long ago, at 97, and my youngest grandchild is now seven - and I love that they have all spent time in the kitchen with me (and eating with me too). Part of the beauty and fun of food for me is, and has always been, enjoying it with loved ones.

In this book I want to turn back time and share all of my favourite family recipes – special dishes that have been handed down to me from my grandmothers, my mother and close friends over the years. You may recognise a few meals in here that remind you of times past and you will soon see that reclaiming a little bit of history is just as simple, just as tasty and just as good as you remember.

Back In The Day

In the 'good old days' processed food did not exist.

People weren't aware of low fat, low sugar or low calories. You didn't have to concern yourself with Paleo, Keto, or any other 'must eat' diet.

Days started early. Breakfast was at 7am; morning tea was at 10am; lunch at noon; afternoon tea at 3:30pm; and dinner (or tea in Australia) was around 6pm.

Only seasonal fruit and vegetables were available so the menu was created accordingly.

Sunday was family day and Sunday lunch was the big meal of the week. Usually a roast after church, the roast was put on before church and then the vegetables added when you got home. This was followed by a special sweet, like steam pudding, lemon meringue pie or apple pie. The leftover cold meat was used for sandwiches or cold meat fritters and any leftover vegetables were used to make bubble and squeak.

During the week, eating was a simple affair and portion sizes were small. Many people simply couldn't afford anything too extravagant and had to purchase what was in season and readily available.

My mother was married during the Second World War. After the war was a recession, which meant a strict budget and living on food rations for a time. Because of this she learnt how to cook with just the basics and managed to turn it into a nourishing, tasty meal. This was a skill that she continued to utilise through most of her life.

Food was never wasted. Old fruit and vegetables were never thrown out and instead made into soup, pies, stews, jams and pickles.

Dad always had a vegetable patch, passionfruit vine and strawberries when in season.

From Mum, I learnt to make a meal from what was in the cupboard or refrigerator. This was very valuable when I got married and had children of my own – especially as my husband always had a habit of inviting someone for a meal at the last minute.

In my early married life, my husband's job meant that we moved often and I joined clubs to meet other women so as not to be lonely. Once again cooking played a big part of my life with cake stalls, progressive dinners and making club cookbooks (filled with our favourite recipes) for charity.

Of course, this was a time when it was expected that women would stay home if they had small children. Today, we have more options with both time, money and food. This is wonderful, but also challenging, as those skills that were once passed around throughout family and community are not as readily available as they once were. More choice also means that we are sometimes overwhelmed with options, and lacking in spare time. It is for all of these reasons that I was keen to share some of the fail-proof recipes that were easy, inexpensive and always a hit throughout the generations.

Grow Your Own

When I was growing up everyone had a vegetable garden and fruit trees even if you only had a small yard. You shared what you grew with your neighbours, often you would work together to grow different food.

You knew where your food came from.

You eggs came from your chooks or from someone you knew. Milk and cream was delivered in glass bottles and you made your own ice cream. Often you made your own bread and all your cakes, scones, slices and biscuits.

You understood every part of the process from growing, to making, to eating.

I firmly believe everyone should grow some of their own food. You don't need much space to grow basics like herbs, tomatoes, capsicum and strawberries. They can even be grown in pots on a balcony and they are all good starters as they are quite hard to kill! A sunny spot, some soil and water is all you need and the joy and pleasure you get from picking and eating your own food is well worth the effort.

Growing your own food will also make you so much more aware of the seasons and what should be available at different times of the year (something that the supermarkets tend to help us forget!) To eat a fruit or vegetable in season is completely different than buying something and eating something out of season. The taste is richer, truer and much, much nicer.

Even those with the biggest and blackest of thumbs can try their hand at growing vegetables and herbs. The following are all relatively simple (love, light and water is all that's required...just like the rest of us!) and can be grown in a small patch in the backyard, or in pots if you don't have a garden:

- Mint
- Parsley
- Basil
- Coriander
- Rosemary
- Nasturtium flowers
- Swiss Chard
- Zucchini
- Lerttuce
- Spinach
- Kale
- Tomato
- Radish
- Squash
- Cucumber
- Onion
- Carrots
- Green beans
- Capsicum
- Chillies
- Pumpkin

Basics

These days, pastry and butter gets a pretty bad wrap. Like all things though, I don't believe there are any 'bad' foods (everything is OK in moderation!) and these are two things that can greatly assist many an otherwise simple meal.

One of the things that is very apparent is that serving sizes these days are huge! Visit an op shop or vintage store and you will see how small the dinner plates used to be, and what was considered a standard serving size.

Stocking A Pantry

When I was a teenager, I attended a Girl's High School, where Home Economics was taught as a subject. I am forever grateful for what I was taught in those classes – meal planning, measurements and quantities, knowing the different cuts of meat and how to cook them, shopping lists and how to stock a pantry.

Cooking is just so much easier (and more fun) if you are organised and prepared in your kitchen.

- Have all your equipment close to hand eg. knife block, blender, food processor, mix master, bowls, measuring cups and spoons, scales ,cooking utensils, saucepans, frying pan, roasting dish, pie dish, casserole dish, cake tins ,oven trays cooling racks, scales, sifter, grater, peeler and rolling pin.
- Buy the freshest food you can find.
- Buy 'little and often' so there isn't any wastage for having out of date items.
- Make the most of seasonal produce.
- Use fresh herbs for more potent flavour. Grow them in pots on your window sill or stand cut bunches in water in a shady spot.
- Use freshly ground black pepper for greater pungency and sea salt as it brings out the flavor of food and you need less –especially if you use a salt mill.
- Read you recipe and make sure you have all your ingredients before you start.
- Keep your kitchen stocked with the basics (the list below is a good start!)

The Pantry:
Flours (self-raising flour, plain flour, corn flour, rice flour)
Sugars (brown, white refined, caster and icing)
Pasta and noodles
Cocoa
Baking powder, bi- carb soda
Vanilla essence
Honey, golden syrup, maple syrup
Sauces (tomato, Tabasco, soy, chilli, worchestershire)
Vinegar (white, cider, balsamic)
Oils (extra virgin olive oil, sunflower oil)
Stock cubes and gravy mix powder
Mustard powder, curry powder
Spices (cumin, cayenne pepper, paprika, coriander, all spice, nutmeg, cinnamon, ground ginger, sea salt, black peppercorns)
Almonds, dried fruit
Jams
Canned fish
Canned tomatoes and beans
Tin foil, cling wrap and greaseproof paper.
Bread

The Refrigerator:
Eggs
Milk
Cream
Cheese
Yoghurt

The Freezer:
Ice- cream
Pre made stock

*To keep pastry:

Pastry not intended for immediate use should be folded in greaseproof paper and kept in refrigerator.

Fats used for shortening are butter, clarified fat, suet and margarine. Always use good quality fat, as the flavour of the pastry is determined by the fat used. Butter is best for a rich pastry, but a mixture of butter and clarified fat or butter and margarine or all margarine is fine.

To give the pastry a nice appearance when cooked brush the top with a liquid – beaten egg and milk or milk alone for meat or vegetable pies.

Fruit pies are glazed with sugar dissolved in water – 1 tablespoon of each.

Pastry

There are a few different types of pastry and each serves a different purpose. There are also some simple rules when it comes to preparing this easy and very versitile basic.

Kinds of Pastry:
Suet crust – used for suet dumplings, boiled jam roly, boiled fruit and meat puddings.
Short crust – used for Cornish pasties and meat and vegetable pies.
Sweet short crust – used for all fruit pies and tarts.
Flaky pastry for meat pies, jam tarts and apple pies.
Rough puff pastry for more elaborate cookery where a flake is required in the pastry.
Puff pastry for elaborate pastry cases.
Choux pastry for cases to hold a sweet filling, as in cream puffs or eclairs, or for small savoury cases.

Pastry, being made of flour and fat, is an energy and heat given food. If it is well made and well baked, it should be well digested by ordinary healthy people, but it should not form an undue proportion of the diet. It is slower to digest than bread, on account of the fat it contains – the particles of flour being surrounded by fat are more slowly digested. Short crust is rather more digestible than flaky pastry, and should be light and crumbly.

Rules For Making Pastry:
1 Use fresh, dry flour. Always sieve it to free it from lumps and to aerate it.
2. Make the pastry in a cool, airy place.
3. When rubbing the fat into the flour use your fingertips, and lift your hands up from the bowl so that the air is caught as the flour falls back into the bowl.
4. Use freshly drawn cold water for mixing and mix with a round-bladed knife. Do not use too much water or the pastry will be hard.
5. Handle the pastry as little as possible. Work quickly.
6. Allow the pastry to stand for a short time in a cool place after making, particularly in hot weather.
7. Roll the pastry lightly, quickly and evenly with short strokes, lifting the rolling pin between each stroke.
8. Always roll away from oneself and never from side to side,
9. Use very little flour for rolling out and remove any surplus flour with a pastry brush.
10. When making puff, flaky or rough puff pastry allow the pastry to relax, if possible for 15 minutes between every two rollings.
11. Put the pastry into a hot oven to cook.
Note: Choux pastry is an exception to these rules.

Short Crust Pastry

This is a savoury pastry suitable for meat, chicken and vegetable pies and a base for quiches etc.

INGREDIENTS
- 250 gm (8oz) plain flour
- 1 teaspoon baking powder
- Pinch salt
- 125 gm (4 oz) cold butter or margarine, cut into small pieces
- 3-5 tablespoons water

METHOD
1. Sift flour, baking powder and salt.
2. Rub fat in with fingertips till the mixture resembles breadcrumbs.
3. Gradually add sufficient water to mix into a firm dough.
4. Turn onto a floured board and work until smooth, without much kneading.
5. Use as required.

Sweet Short Pastry

As the name reflects, there's sugar added for a little extra sweetness with this one. This pastry can be used for sweet jam tarts or any fruit pie.

INGREDIENTS
- 250gm (8 oz) plain flour
- Pinch salt
- 125gm (4oz) butter
- 90gm (3oz) castor sugar
- 1 egg yolk
- 2 tablespoons milk

METHOD
1. Sift the flour and the salt into a bowl.
2. Using the tips of your finger rub the butter into the flour until it resembles breadcrumbs.
3. Add the sugar, egg yolk and milk into the flour and fat blend, using a fork until the mixture clings together in a ball, leaving the sides of the mixing bowl.
4. Turn the dough onto a lightly floured surface and knead lightly to make a smooth fairly stiff dough.
5. Wrap the pastry in cling wrap and set to rest in the refrigerator until required.

Herb Butter

Herbed butters were often used on top of a lamb chop or a piece of steak in lieu of sauce. Any herb growing in the garden can be used as a herbed butter - but if you're serving lamb, then it's nice to add mint.

INGREDIENTS
- 4 tablespoon butter (softened)
- 1 tablespoon each of fresh mint, parsley and sage (finely chopped)

METHOD
1. Mix all the ingredients together.
2. Store in a covered container in the refrigerator.

Garlic Butter

Garlic has always been used as a flavour enhancer and we were always told how good it was for the immune system. Stale bread was brought to life with garlic butter - buttered, wrapped in tin foil and heated in the oven.

INGREDIENTS
- 4 tablespoon butter (softened)
- 1 tablespoon fresh finely chopped parsley
- 1 tablespoon fresh finely chopped chives
- 3 cloves of garlic, peeled and minced

METHOD
1. Mix all the ingredients together.
2. Store in a covered container in the refrigerator.

Soups & Starters

You will quickly see that many of the recipes in this section make excellent use of leftovers - particularly leftovers from those recipes used in the 'mains' section. There is an incredible amount of waste these days and this was something that my parents and grandparents simply couldn't afford. So, extra meat or not-so-pretty vege became soups and starters!

Pea & Ham Soup

Pea and ham soup was often used as an inexpensive meal. Rich, thick and filling, this soup made use of a cheap hock from the butchers and some leftover vegetables.

INGREDIENTS
- 1 cup split green dried peas
- 1 cup dried peas
- 1 cup diced carrot
- 1 cup diced celery
- 1 large brown onion or ½ a leek
- 1 beef stock cube
- 1 large smoked ham hock
- Salt and pepper to taste
- Cold water (approximately 10-12 cups)

METHOD
1. Place dried and split peas in a large bowl and cover with water and let soak overnight.
2. Place ham hock in a large stockpot and put in enough water to cover the hock.
3. Place pot on the stove and slowly bring water to the boil, then simmer for an hour until the meat is soft on the bone.
4. Allow to cool then skim off fat from the top.
5. Remove hock from the liquid, remove the meat from the bone, cut up and put aside.
6. Add the drained dried and split peas, onion (or leek), celery, carrot, and beef stock cube to the liquid.
7. Bring to the boil and then simmer for 30 minutes.
8. Add the hock meat and simmer for another 10 minutes.
9. Season with salt and pepper if required.

*Keeps well in the refrigerator for 7 days.

*Serve with fresh crusty bread or a French breadstick, sliced and spread with garlic butter (page 22) or herbed butter (page 21) which is then wrapped with tin foil and warmed in the oven.

*This soup gets thicker and has more flavour from the second day.

Lamb & Vege Soup

Lamb shanks are quite fashionable these days, but a shank used to be a very cheap cut of meat. This, combined with all your old vegetables, resulted in a hearty, filling soup that made a meal all of its own.

INGREDIENTS
- 2 lamb shanks
- 1 tablespoon olive oil
- 2 onions, peeled and chopped
- 1 clove garlic, crushed
- 2 sticks celery
- 2 carrots, peeled and chopped
- 2 potatoes, peeled and chopped
- 1 turnip, peeled and chopped
- 1 parsnip, peeled and chopped
- 2 beef stock cubes
- 1 litre (1 ¾ pints) water
- ½ cup pearl barley or rice
- 2 bay leaves

METHOD
1. Put the olive oil into a large pot.
2. Add the lamb shanks and brown them.
3. Remove the shanks and put aside.
4. Add the onion and garlic to the oil and cook for 2 minutes.
5. Add the chopped vegetables, water, crumbled stock cubes, lamb shanks, bay leaves and pearl barley. If you would prefer rice DO NOT put this into the pot yet as it does not take long to cook.
6. Slowly bring to the boil, cover pot with lid and simmer for 1 ½ hour or until pearl barley is tender and the meat is starting to fall off the bone.
7. Remove the shanks from the pot and remove the meat from the bones.
8. Roughly chop the meat and return it to the pot with rice, if you are having rice instead of barley.
9. Simmer for a further 15 to 20 minutes.

*Serve with fresh chunky bread or a French-stick sliced and spread with garlic butter (page 22) or herbed butter (page 21), wrap in tin foil and heat in the oven.

Chicken Broth

This is a recipe for both chicken stock, and chicken broth
(or a thin, light chicken soup).
When ever I cook or buy a full roasted chicken, I never throw away
the carcass as it makes great chicken stock.

INGREDIENTS

Stock:
- 1 cooked chicken carcass, removed of any stuffing , if the cooked chicken had stuffing inside it.
- 6 cups of water
- ½ cup finely diced carrot
- 1 carrot roughly chopped
- 1 onion roughly chopped
- 2 sticks celery
- 1 sachet bouquet garni

Broth:
- ½ cup finely diced carrot
- ½ cup finely diced celery
- 1 finely diced medium onion
- ¼ cup uncooked rice
- 1 tablespoon finely chopped fresh parsley
- 4 cups of chicken stock
- ½ to 1 cup of chopped cooked chicken.
Salt and pepper to taste

METHOD

Stock:
1. Put the chicken carcass in a large pot and cover it with water. Place the lid on the pot, and put it onto the hot plate turned high, bring the water to the boil, then turn heat down to low and simmer for 2 hours.
2. Strain the liquid off and put to one side. 4 cups can be used for making the chicken broth and any remaining stock can be placed in 1 cup containers for the freezer to use for other meals.
3. Remove any chicken meat off the carcass and put the meat into the refrigerator.

Broth:
1. Place the vegetables, stock and rice into a large pot, cover, and simmer gently for 40 to 60 minutes.
2. Add the chicken pieces and seasonings and cook until chicken is heated.

*Serve with hot crusty bread spread with garlic butter (page 22)

*For generations this Chicken Broth has been a family favourite - lovely on a cold winter day or night and a must whenever you had a cold. It was meant to be a sure cure, I don't know if it cured your cold, but is certainly soothed it and was a great help.

Savoury Scones

These were initially a way for me to get my fussy kids to eat more vegetables! Quick, easy and tasty, these scones are great because you don't need to be too fussy about measurements. Near enough is good enough with this recipe - both with regards to ingredients and mixture on the pan!

INGREDIENTS
- 2 cups Self-raising flour
- 1 tablespoon butter
- 1 peeled and grated carrot
- 1 peeled and grated onion
- 60gm (2 oz) grated tasty cheese
- 1 tablespoon freshly chopped parsley
- 1 egg
- Milk

METHOD
1. Preheat oven 200 degrees C (400 degrees F).
2. Grease 2 oven trays.
3. In a large mixing bowl rub the butter into the flour with your fingertips.
4. Add the carrot, onion, cheese and parsley, then break one egg into a cup and beat slightly, fill the cup with milk and beat the egg and milk together.
5. Pour the egg and milk mixture into the flour and other ingredients and mix well.
6. Drop dessert-spoonfuls of the mixture onto the greased trays.
7. Bake 10-12 minutes in the oven until golden or until they lift off and don't stick to the tray.

*Wrap in a tea-towel to keep warm

*Serve hot or cold, spread with butter if desired.

Bacon Scone Roll

When we were at school, we were lucky to come home for lunch and this was often what we ate. Quick, easy and inexpensive, it is the perfect snack!

INGREDIENTS
Pastry:
- 3 cups Self-raising flour
Pinch cayenne pepper
1 teaspoon salt
60 gm (3 oz) butter
1 cup milk

Filling:
2 rashers of bacon, rind removed, diced and cooked
1 cup grated tasty cheddar cheese
1 tablespoon grain mustard
½ teaspoon paprika
1 egg, beaten to glaze
1 cup milk

METHOD
1. Preheat oven to 200 degrees C (400 degrees F).
2. Lightly grease an oven tray.
3. Sift flour, cayenne pepper and salt into a large mixing bowl.
4. Rub the butter into the flour with your fingertips until it resembles breadcrumbs.
5. Make a well in the centre and gradually add milk, mixing with a fork to make a soft dough.
6. Turn dough out onto a floured board and knead.
7. Roll out dough to form a rectangle, 30cm x25c, (12 x 10 inches).
8. Combine filling ingredients and sprinkle over the dough, leaving a 2.5 cm (1 inch) border around the edges.
9. Moisten the edges with a little milk.
10. Starting at the longest edge, roll up like a Swiss roll, to enclose the filling.
11. Place seam side down, onto the baking tray.
12. Lightly brush with beaten egg.
13. Bake for approximately 20 minutes until the roll is risen and golden brown.

Serve hot, cut into slices.

Bubble & Squeak

My grandmother was English and Bubble and Squeak was a traditional British breakfast dish made with shallow fried left over vegetables from roast dinner. The dish was maned from the noise the cabbage makes bubbling and squeaking during the cooking process.

INGREDIENTS
- Any left over vegetables (eg. peas, beans, pumpkin, carrot, corn, cabbage or brussell sprouts etc.)
- Extra cooked mashed potatoes.

METHOD
1. Put potatoes and left over vegetables in a mixing bowl.
2. Mix together with a little butter, salt and pepper.
3. Melt some butter in a frying pan.
4. Spread the vegetables into the frying pan, (mixture should be approximately 3cm (1 ½ inches) deep) and fry gently until one side is golden and crisp .
5. Turn out onto a serving plate and cut into slices or cut with a scone cutter.

Cold Meat Fritters

After our Sunday Roast for lunch (then cold meat and salad or cold meat and vegetables for the evening meal) the meat that was left over was then used for sandwiches and cold meat fritters.

INGREDIENTS
- 375gm (12 oz) leftover cooked meat
- 1 tablespoon chopped fresh parsley
- ½ teaspoon salt
- Pinch of pepper
- 1 cup S.R. Flour
- 1 egg
- ½ cup milk
- a squeeze of lemon juice

METHOD
1. Cut the meat into 6 mm (¼ inch) thick slices and set meat aside.
2. In a bowl place sifted flour, salt, pepper and parsley.
3. Beat egg with a fork in a small bowl or cup, add milk and lemon juice and mix together.
4. Slowly add this mixture into dry mixture to form a dropping consistency.
5. Heat enough oil to cover the surface of a frying pan.
6. Dip meat into the batter mixture and then drop into the oil, allow to cook until golden, then flip and cook the other side.

*Serve with tomato sauce or relish.

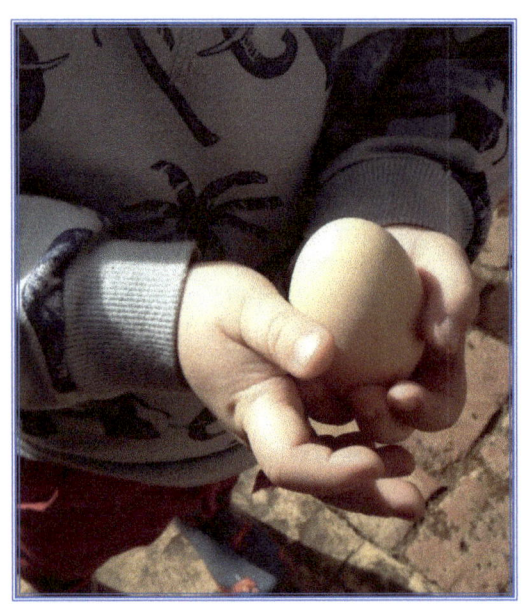

Sauces

It really took multi-culturalism post-World War II to open up people's minds about the endless possibilities of flavour. Until then simple sauces, such as relish and gravy, were what made meals interesting and extra tasty. Aren't we lucky now, to have all the options!

Mayonnaise

The perfect base for lots of creamy sauces. many people these days can't enjoy a sandwich without mayo. A couple of generations back though. it was mainly enjoyed with salads and my mother used to make a recipe containing a lot of condensed milk!

INGREDIENTS
- 2 egg yolks
- ½ teaspoon prepared mustard
- salt and pepper
- 1 cup olive oil
- 2 tablespoon lemon juice

METHOD
1. Whisk egg yolks, mustard and salt and pepper until sticky.
2. Gradually add ¼ cup oil, drop by drop, whisking constantly. If preferred, use a blender or food processor.
3. Add 1 tablespoon lemon juice and stir to combine.
4. Pour in remaining oil in a very thin, steady stream, whisking constantly.
5. Stop occasionally to check consistency.

*When all the oil is added, taste and adjust seasoning with salt, pepper and lemon juice.

*It is important that all ingredients are at room temperature

Aioli

This is making a resurgence in restaurants today but in the 1960s we used it as a side with vegetables.

INGREDIENTS
- 1 cup mayonnaise (page 43)
- 2 fresh garlic cloves, crushed
- 1 teaspoon freshly squeezed lemon juice

METHOD
1. In a small bowl combine all the ingredients, and mix.
2. Cover with plastic cling wrap and chill in the refrigerator.
3. Chill for several hours to allow flavours to blend and mellow.

*This is delicious and wonderful as a dip, sandwich spread or as an accompaniment with fish, eggs, meat, potatoes, chicken and salad.

Tartare Sauce

This a perfect sauce to serve with any fish dish, as the tangy flavour enhances the taste of fish.

INGREDIENTS
- 1 cup of mayonnaise (page 43)
- 2 teaspoons capers, drained and finely chopped
- 2 gherkins, finely chopped
- Finely grated rind of 1 lemon
- 2 tablespoon freshly chopped parsley

METHOD
1. Place all ingredients in a bowl and mix.
2. Cover with plastic cling wrap and refrigerate until ready to serve.

Seafood Sauce

A bitter, sweet sauce that gives a tasty finish to a prawn cocktail or used as a dipping sauce with fresh seafood.

INGREDIENTS
- ¼ cup tomato sauce
- 1 teaspoon worcestershire sauce
- ½ cup mayonnaise (page 43)
- ¼ cup thickened cream
- A few drops Tabasco sauce
- Juice of 1 lemon

METHOD
1. In a mixing bowl, combine all the ingredients.
2. Cover with plastic cling wrap and store in the refrigerator until required.

Mushroom Sauce

A great topping on steak, schnitzel and lamb chops, this is a simple sauce that is packed with flavour.

INGREDIENTS
- 1 tablespoon olive oil
- 1 small red onion, peeled and diced
- 250g (8 oz) button mushrooms, sliced
- 1 clove of garlic, peeled and minced
- 4 springs of fresh thyme, finely chopped
- ½ cup sweet sherry
- ½ teaspoon white wine vinegar
- 60 ml (2 fluid oz) cream
- Salt and pepper, to season

METHOD
1. Heat oil in a large heavy based pan over high heat.
2. Add onion and cook for 2 minutes or until softened.
3. Add mushrooms and cook for 8-10 minutes or until mushrooms begin to brown.
4. Stir in garlic and thyme, cook for 1 minute, then add sherry and vinegar.
5. Reduce heat and simmer until mixture is reduced by half, then stir in the cream.
6. When sauce begins to thicken, season with salt and pepper.
7. Serve.

Pepper Sauce

A great accompaniment to serve with t-bone steak. this sauce is delicious with any meat dish.

INGREDIENTS
- 2-3 tablespoons of whole black peppercorns
- 60 gm (2 oz) butter
- 2 spring onions, chopped
- 100 ml (3 fluid oz) brandy
- 100 ml (3 fluid oz) hot water
- 1 beef stock cube, crumbled
- 60 ml (2 fluid oz) cream
- Pinch salt

METHOD
1. Crush the peppercorns with a mortar and pestle or a rolling pin.
2. Melt the butter in a saucepan, then add the spring onion and cook until soft.
3. Add brandy and peppercorns and boil for 3 minutes.
4. Mix crumbled beef stock cube in to the hot water, then add to pot and boil another 3 minutes.
5. Reduce the heat and add the cream, heat through but DO NOT BOIL, until the sauce is the right thickness.

Mustard Sauce

The perfect sauce to serve with silverside or corned beef. I also love this one with baked salmon!

INGREDIENTS
- 1 egg
- 1 level tablespoon dry mustard
- 3 dessertspoons sugar
- ½ cup vinegar
- ½ cup liquid from the meat (see page 75)
- salt and pepper to taste

METHOD
1. In a small saucepan beat the egg well and mix with the mustard and sugar.
2. Blend in the vinegar and liquid from the meat.
3. Stir over gentle heat until thickened DO NOT LET IT BOIL.
4. Add a little salt and pepper to taste.
5. Remove the meat from the liquid and drain.
6. Strain off the liquid over a colindar to catch the vegetables.
7. Cut the meat onto serving plates with the vegetables. Top the meat with mustard sauce.

Red Wine Sauce

A delicious sauce to serve with roast meat or steak.

INGREDIENTS
- 30 g (1oz) butter
- 1 medium brown onion peeled and chopped
- 1 clove of garlic, peeled and crushed
- ½ cup dry red wine
- 1 cup hot water
- 1 beef stock cube, crushed

METHOD
1. Melt the butter in a pan over medium heat.
2. Add onion, cook until softened.
3. Add garlic, cook for a further 1 minute stirring all the time.
4. Add wine and bring to the boil.
5. Reduce heat and simmer for 3-5 minutes.
6. Mix crushed beef cube into the hot water and then add to the pan.
7. Bring to the boil.
8. Reduce heat and simmer for 10-12 minutes or until sauce thickens.

Mains

Main dishes are mostly hot and based on fish, meat and poultry. Meat is hearty and satisfying and, when served with vegetables, highly nutritious. For generations, the traditional Sunday roast was the highlight of a family meal and a weekly treat. A casserole or pie is welcome in the winter and cold meat is enjoyed with salad in the summer.

Cornish Pasty

This was the first recipe that I was taught to cook at school (pastry, and then Cornish Pasties). Everyone in my family has always loved them and they are a fabulous nutritious meal on their own (with tomato sauce...of course!)

INGREDIENTS
- 250gm (8oz) short crust pastry (page 18)
- 250gm (8oz) steak (shoulder blade, skirt, chuck or round)
- 1 potato
- ½ turnip
- 1 onion
- 1 tablespoon fresh parsley, finely chopped
- Salt and pepper to taste

METHOD
1. Heat oven to moderately hot 180-190 degrees C (350-375 degrees F).
2. Cut the steak finely into 1cm (1/2 inch) pieces.
3. Peel and dice the vegetables into 1cm (1/2nch) pieces.
4. Put the meat and vegetables into a large bowl, add the salt and pepper and parsley. Moisten all the ingredients with a little water.
5. Prepare the pastry and divide in half, then divide each half into four equal pieces.
6. This will give you eight pieces.
7. Roll out each part into a round the size of a saucer.
8. Divide the meat mixture between the rounds.
9. Brush the edges with water, close; and shape into pasties.
10. Glaze with a mixture of egg and milk or just milk.
11. Place on a cold tray and bake in the oven for 30-40 minutes.

*The traditional Cornish Pasties only use white vegetables but over the years to help little children to eat more vegetables ,or to use up left over vegetables, I have added other vegetables to the mix but then they are just called pasties.

Steak & Kidney Pie

My granny used to make a wonderful steak and kidney pie and back in her day she would have used lard instead of butter in her pastry. It was a favourite recipe for my mum as well and she much preferred sheep's kidney as opposed to the ox kidney that was popular back in the 30s and 40s.

INGREDIENTS
- Double quantity of Shortcrust Pastry (page 18)
- 500 g (16 oz or 1 lb) steak
- 4 sheep's kidneys
- 4 tablespoon plain flour
- ½ teaspoon salt
- Pinch of pepper
- 2 tablespoons chopped onion
- 2 tablespoon chopped bacon
- 2 cups hot water
- 1 crushed beef stock cube
- 3 tablespoons olive oil
- Egg yolk or milk for glazing

METHOD
1. Cut steak into 2.5 cm (1 inch) cubes.
2. Wash and skin the kidneys and cut into small pieces.
3. Mix flour, salt and pepper on a plate and roll cubes of steak and kidney in it.
4. Place olive oil in a large heavy based pot, add steak and kidney in batches, and cook until brown.
5. Remove the steak and kidney from the pan, set aside.
6. Add remaining oil to pot and add bacon and onions to it, cook until soft.
7. Return steak and kidney to pot with water and crushed stock cube.
8. Bring to the boil, then reduce heat to low.
9. Cover the pot and simmer for 1 hour or until steak is tender
10. Remove from heat. Refrigerate for 3 hours or until completely cool.
11. Preheat oven to 220 degrees C or 425 degrees F
12. To make individual pies divide the dough into 12 pieces and roll each piece into a circular shape for the top and bottom of the pies.
13. Line the bottom and sides of each tin with pastry.
14. Divide the steak and kidney mixture between each pie.
15. Brush the edges with water.
16. Place the top of the pastry over the mixture and press down firmly around the edges to seal. Trim.
17. With a sharp knife cut a couple of slits into the top of the pastry on each pie.
18. Brush the top of each pie with beaten egg.
19. Place pies into the preheated oven for 10 minutes then turn down the temperature to 190 degrees C or 375 degrees C for a further 20 minutes until the pastry is golden brown.

Chicken Mushroom Pie

A delicious melt-in-your-mouth pie. this simple pie is full of flavour.

INGREDIENTS
- 2 chicken breasts
- 2 tablespoons oil
- 375 g (12 oz) button mushrooms
- 1 medium brown onion peeled and diced
- 2 tablespoons cornflour
- 1 cup (250 ml / 8 fl oz) chicken stock
salt and pepper to taste
- 2 tablespoons fresh parsley finely chopped
- 1 egg, beaten for glazing
- 1 quanity of short crust pastry (page 18)

METHOD
1. Preheat oven to 200 degrees C (400 degrees F).
2. Cut chicken into bite size pieces.
3. Heat oil in a pan and brown chicken pieces for 10 minutes.
4. Add mushrooms and onions and stir until lightly browned.
5. Stir in tomatoes. Sprinkle in flour then gradually pour in the chicken stock.
6. Season with salt and pepper to taste and add parsley, stir in.
7. Remove pan from heat and set aside.
8. Make the pastry as per recipe on page 18.
9. Roll out 2/3 rds of the pastry onto a floured board to 5mm (1/2 inch) and line a 20cm (8 inch) pie plate with pastry.
10. Fill the pie crust with the chicken and mushroom mixture filling.
11. Roll out remaining pastry to form a lid.
12. Cover the pie and seal edges with a little cold water.
13. Make leaves out of the left over pastry and put on top of the pie.
14. Brush pie with beaten egg.
15. Bake for 30-40 minutes or until pie is golden brown.

Serves 6

Egg & Bacon Pie

Before quiche was popular (or even really known!) people still enjoyed an egg and bacon pie - a lot less work, and just as tasty!

INGREDIENTS
- 250g (8oz) of prepared Short Crust Pastry (page 18)
- 90gm (3oz) bacon
- 3 eggs
- 1 teaspoon parsley, finely chopped
- Salt and pepper

METHOD
1. Heat the oven to moderately hot 200 degrees C (400 degrees F).
2. Cut the rind off the bacon and cut the bacon into 5cm (2 inch) pieces.
3. Put the bacon into a small saucepan, cover with cold water and bring to the boil.
4. Strain off the water.
5. Divide the pastry into two equal parts.
6. Roll out one half and line a pie dish with the pastry.
7. Place the bacon and parsley into the pie dish, break the eggs over the bacon.
8. Season with salt and pepper.
9. Roll out the other half of the pastry and place on top of the pie.
10. Pinch the pastry edges together.
11. Brush the top of the pie with a mixture of egg and milk or milk.
12. Bake in a moderately hot oven for 10 minutes then turn the oven down to slow 150 degrees C (300 degrees F) for a further 20 minutes.

Cheese & Tomato Flan

I met a friend back in the early 1970s who used to call this a 'man's quiche' and she was right...even those who don't consider quiche much of a meal seem to enjoy this one!

INGREDIENTS
- 125gm (4oz) Shortcrust pastry (page 18)
- 1 ½ cups grated tasty cheese
- 1 white onion, finely chopped
- ½ teaspoon dried oregano
- 90gm (3 oz) salami thinly sliced
- 155gm (5 oz) can tomato paste
- Pinch salt
- Pepper to taste
- 3 tablespoons water
- 1 egg, lightly beaten

METHOD
1. Preheat oven to 230 degrees C (450 degrees F).
2. Roll out the prepared pastry and line a flan dish with the pastry.
3. Sprinkle half the cheese on top of the pastry, then add the onion and oregano.
4. Place on the slices of salami.
5. Mix the tomato paste, water, salt and pepper and spoon over evenly.
6. Pour over the beaten egg.
7. Finish by sprinkling on remaining cheese.
8. Bake for 15 minutes then reduce heat to 190 degrees C (375 degrees F) for a further 15 minutes.

Roast Pork

Roast Pork always reminds me of Christmas, sitting around the dining table with your family and extended family - happy times and lovely memories.

INGREDIENTS
- 1 x 1.5 kg (3 lb) leg of Pork (make sure the butcher has scored the skin for you)
- Olive oil
- Sea salt
- Vegetables for Roasting eg potato, pumpkin, parsnip, carrot and brown onion

APPLE SAUCE:
- 4 large granny smith apples
- ½ cup brown sugar
- ¾ cup water
- juice of 1 lemon
- pinch of cinnamon and mixed spice

GRAVY:
- 2 tablespoons roast fat/oil
- 1 tablespoon flour
- 1 cup of stock or water

METHOD
1. Preheat oven to 220 degress C (400 degrees F). Cooking time – allow 30-35 minutes per 500g (1lb) plus an extra 30 minutes for the piece.
2. Pat the leg of pork with paper towel to remove as much moisture as possible. This will give a better crackle.
3. Rub olive oil over and into the skin, then sprinkle sea salt generously over the olive oil.
4. Place the leg of pork into a roasting pan that has the base covered with olive oil.
5. Put the pork into a very hot oven for 20 minutes (this allows the pork rind to crackle), turning your baking pan around once to allow crackle on both sides.
6. Then lower oven to 150 degrees C (325 degrees F) for remaining time of cooking.
7. Put in your vegetables 1 hour before the finished cooking time, (turning them ½ an hour later, so as both sides are cooked.

APPLE SAUCE:
1. Peel and chop the apples.
2. Place in a saucepan with the water, lemon juice and cinnamon and mixed spice.
3. Simmer until the apples are tender and the liquid is reduced, about 30minutes.
4. Puree until smooth.

GRAVY:
1. Drain off most of the fat/oil from the roasting pan, leaving approx. 2 tablespoons with sediment.
2. Sprinkle the flour into the oil, stir well to remove lumps.
3. Place pan on stove (medium heat), stir until flour starts to colour. Take off heat and gradually add stock/water to pan. Return to heat and stir until gravy thickens and bubbles. Season to taste.

Silverside

In mum's day, corned beef was the cheap piece of the beef rolled and corned. Over the years we've become fussy and modern day silverside is virtually fat free. Silverside was always a little expensive two generations back and was considered a real treat.

INGREDIENTS
- 1 kg (2 lb) piece of corned beef or silverside
- 1 tablespoon sugar
- 2 tablespoon white vinegar
- 2 bay leaves
- 6 black whole peppercorns
- Mustard sauce (page 55)

METHOD
1. Place the corned silverside in a large heavy based saucepan or stock pot and barely cover with cold water.
2. Add the sugar, vinegar, bay leaves and peppercorns.
3. Cover and bring slowly boiling , then turn heat to simmer and keep simmering.
4. When there is only about ¾ of an hour of cooking time left (see below for estimates), I add peeled and halved potatoes, peeled and halved carrots, and peeled quarters of sweet corn.
5. 15 minutes before the end of cooking time I add whole sliced top and tailed beans.
6. Ten minutes before the end of cooking time I make the mustard sauce (go to page 55 for the recipe).

*Allowing 30 minutes per 500gm (1lb) and 30 minutes over, until meat is tender.
So for a 1 kg (2lb) piece that would be 1 ½ hours.

*If you want this as a main meal, I cook my vegetables in the pot at the same time.

Baked Stuffed Topside

This topside roast is very tasty and tender, delicious hot or cold.

INGREDIENTS
- 1.5kg (3lb) corner cut topside
- 2 tablespoons olive oil
- 2 tablespoon water

Stuffing:
- 2 cups soft white breadcrumbs
- 1 tablespoon butter
- 1 small onion, peeled
- and finely chopped
- 1 teaspoon grated lemon rind
- Salt and pepper
- ½ teaspoon mixed herbs
- 1 egg beaten

METHOD
1. Preheat oven to moderate 180 degrees C (350 degrees F).
2. Place breadcrumbs in a basin and rub in the butter.
3. Add the remaining of the ingredients and bind together with the egg.
4. Cut a pocket in the steak and fill with the stuffing.
5. Secure opening with wooden cocktail sticks or fine skewers and bind with cotton.
6. Heat oil in roasting pan on the stove on medium heat, brown meat all over.
7. Add water and cover pan.
8. Place roast in the oven and bake one and a half hours or until tender.
9. Vegetables such as potatoes, pumpkin, carrots can be added to the pan an hour before the meat is cooked.
10. Remove the roast and vegetables from the pan and place on ovenproof dishes and place back in the oven on a low temperature to keep warm.
11. Make gravy from pan juices, see page 71, and serve with roast vegetables and a green vegetable.

Carpet Bag Steak

An easy, delicious recipe which is full of flavour, as the oysters soak up some of the juice from the steak and vice versa.

INGREDIENTS
- 20 g butter
- 8 fresh rock oysters, shucked
- 4 eye fillet steaks (220g)
- Sea salt and freshly crushed black pepper
- 1 tablespoon olive oil

METHOD
1. Preheat oven to 200 degrees Celcius (400 degrees F).
2. Line an ovenproof tray with baking paper or foil.
3. Cut a 3cm wide pocket in side of each side of steak to fit oysters, ensuring knife does not piece all the way through.
4. Fill each pocket with 2 oysters. Secure with toothpicks.
5. Season with salt and pepper.
6. Heat oil and butter in a large frypan, on high heat.
7. Sear steaks 2 minutes on each side.
8. Transfer steak to tray.
9. Bake 5-6 minutes for medium or until cooked to your liking.
10. Remove from oven, rest, with the steak covered loosely with foil.
11. Accompany with shoe string fries, a fresh green salad and crunchy bread.

Beef Burgundy

At school, as part of our cooking classes, we were given the task of cooking meals from all different countries. What fun we had going through the recipe books! This was an easy French recipe, one that I still use all the time.

INGREDIENTS
- 500 gm (1 lb) bladebone steak
- 4 small brown onions, peeled and halved
- 2 medium carrots, peeled and sliced
- 125gm (4 oz) bacon
- 1 cup hot water
- 1 beef stock cube
- 2 tablespoons plain flour
- 1 cup red wine
- 3 tablespoons olive oil
- 50gm butter
- Bouquet Garni sachet
- Salt and pepper

METHOD
1. Preheat oven to 160 degrees C (350 degrees F).
2. Cut steak into 3cm (1 inch) cubes, toss in flour that has been seasoned with salt and pepper.
3. Heat 1 tablespoon of the oil in a large heavy bottomed pot.
4. Cut bacon into cubes and fry, drain and put aside.
5. Add remaining oil and butter into pot and fry meat in small batches until browned.
6. Remove meat from pan and put into a casserole dish.
7. Fry onions until browned, remove onions from pan and put with bacon.
8. Add carrots and fry a further two minutes.
9. Add wine and water, crushed stock cube and seasoning.
10. Put onions, bacon and carrot on top of beef in casserole dish.
11. Pour liquid on top.
12. Cover the casserole with lid and bake in a moderate oven for 1-1 ½ hours.

Serves 4

Herb Lamb Rack

A great dish for entertaining that has restaurant quality. Impress your friends with this juicy rack of lamb. they will never guess how easy it is to make.

INGREDIENTS
- 2 tablespoons chopped parsley
- 1 tablespoon chopped spring onion (scallions)
- 1 clove garlic, crushed
- 1 teaspoon finely chopped rosemary
- ½ cup fresh bread crumbs
- 15g (½ oz) melted butter
- Salt and pepper
- 15g (½ oz) butter extra
- Rosemary sprigs to garnish
- 1 tablespoon olive oil

METHOD
1. Heat oven to 220 degrees C (425 degrees F).
2. Combine parsley, spring onions, garlic, rosemary and breadcrumbs and butter in a bowl.
3. Sprinkle lamb with salt and pepper.
4. Put olive oil in a roasting pan on the stove top, add lamb and brown lamb evenly all over.
5. Take off heat.
6. Cover lamb racks with herb mixture.
7. Bake in the oven for 15 minutes.
8. Serve with mint sauce and vegetables of your choice.

Garnish with sprigs of rosemary.

Serves 2

Veal Cordon Bleu

Cordon bleu is French for blue ribbon, which was the highest order under the bourbon kings. It has since been used for first class distinctions in regards to chefs. The term has since applied to food prepared to a very high standard and by outstanding cooks. This dish is certainly a blue ribbon meal.

INGREDIENTS
- 6 veal steaks (cut thin as for schnitzel)
- 6 thin slices of ham
- 6 thin slices of gruyere cheese
- 1 egg (beaten)
- Plain flour seasoned with salt and pepper
- Fine dry breadcrumbs
- 2 oz butter
- 2 tablespoons oil

METHOD
1. Pound steaks, if necessary, until very thin. Top each steak with a slice of ham and a slice of gruyere cheese.
2. Fold steaks in half, secure with small wooden toothpicks.
3. Dip in seasoned flour and beaten egg then press into the breadcrumbs.
4. Refrigerate for 1 hour.
5. Heat butter and oil in large frying pan.
6. Cook steaks, turning occasionally, until cooked through and golden.
7. Drain well, remove tooth picks before serving.

*Serves 6.

Tuna Rice Slice

This recipe is handy when you have very little in your frig and you have to rely on something from your pantry to whip up into a cost saving meal.

INGREDIENTS
- 1 cup rice
- 1 egg, lightly beaten
- 1 small onion, peel and finely chopped
- 180 g (6 oz) can tuna
- 30g (1 oz) butter, melted
- 3 tablespoons plain flour
- 1 teaspoon paprika
- 1 tablespoon chopped parsley
- 2 teaspoons lemon juice
- 30g (1 oz) butter, extra
- 2 cups milk
- 1 teaspoon dry mustard
- 60g (2 oz) tasty cheese, grated
- 1 egg, extra

METHOD
1. Preheat oven to 160 degrees C (350 degrees F).
2. Grease a slice tin.
3. Cook rice in boiling, salted water until tender, drain.
4. In a bowl, combine rice, onion, butter and egg.
5. Press rice mixture over the base and side of a slice tin.
6. Drain the tin of tuna (reserve the liquid and put to one side) spread the flaked tuna over the rice base.
7. In a saucepan, melt the extra butter, then remove from heat.
8. Stir in the flour, working until smooth.
9. Return to heat, add the milk and tuna liquid slowly, stirring constantly until boiling.
10. Reduce the heat, add mustard, paprika, grated cheese, parsley and lemon juice, stir until the cheese melts.
11. Allow the sauce to cool a little then stir in the extra egg which has been lightly beaten.
12. Spoon the sauce mixture over the tuna.
13. Bake in a moderate oven for 45-50 minutes, or until sauce is quite firm and golden.
14. Serve hot or cold, cut into slices.

Farmers Chicken Casserole

This is a lovely meal and well worth the preparation work, as all the vegetables are in it though you can serve it with a green vegetable if required.

INGREDIENTS
- 2 chicken breasts fillets, cut into 5cm (2 inches) pieces
- ½ cup cornflour
- salt and pepper to taste
- 60 g (2 oz) butter
- 2 tablespoons olive oil
- 3 potatoes, peeled and quartered
- 1 large carrot, peeled and sliced
- 1 parsnip, peeled and sliced
- 1 clove garlic, peeled and crushed
- 1 tablespoon tomato paste
- 2 rashers of bacon, rind removed and cut into pieces
- ½ cup halved button mushrooms
- 2 onions, peeled and chopped
- 1 ½ cups hot water
- 1 chicken stock cube, crushed
- 1 tablespoon freshly cut parsley

METHOD
1. Preheat oven to 190 degrees C (375 degrees F).
2. Season cornflour with salt and pepper.
3. Coat chicken pieces in seasoned cornflour.
4. Heat butter and oil in a heavy based pan and fry chicken pieces until golden.
5. Remove chicken from pan and place in an ovenproof casserole with potato, carrot and parsnip.
6. Add bacon, mushrooms, garlic and onions to the pan and cook 3-4 minutes or until soft.
7. Add crushed chicken stock cube to hot water and mix then pour into pan.
8. Then add tomato paste and mix through.
9. Bring to boiling, stirring constantly.
10. Pour over chicken pieces and potatoes in the casserole dish. Cover and bake in the preheated oven for 1 hour or until the chicken is tender.
11. Sprinkle casserole with chopped parsley before serving.

*Serves 4

Baked Lamb Chops

This dish is quick an easy to cook. a recipe that your family will enjoy. Any lamb chops can be used just remember to cut off any fat.

INGREDIENTS
- 6 chump chops
- 2 tablespoons plain flour seasoned with salt and pepper
- 1 large onion peeled and sliced
- 1 ½ teaspoons brown sugar
- 4 tablespoons tomato sauce
- 1 tablespoon Worcestershire sauce
- ½ teaspoon dried thyme
- 1 tablespoon vinegar
- 1 ½ cups water
- 1 chicken stock cube, crumbled
- Olive oil

METHOD
1. Preheat oven to 180 degrees C or 350 degrees F.
2. Trim excess fat from chops, dredge in seasoned flour.
3. Heat enough oil to cover the bottom of a large heavy based pan, add cops and brown on both sides.
4. Place chops in a oven proof casserole dish. Remove from pan and add the onion and cook until soft.
5. Add sugar, sauces, thyme, vinegar and chicken stock cube that has been mixed with the hot water, stir until well combined .
6. Pour into the casserole dish, cover and put into the preheated oven for 45 minutes of until the chops are tender.

Vegetables

Vegetables are a great accompaniment to a main meal. However, they also take on an interesting finish when added into a sauce or mixed with breadcrumbs, herbs, spices and cheese they make an excellent first course or a tasty vegetarian meal.

Scalloped Potatoes

By the late 60s and early 70s we were buying recipes, trying foods from other countries and having dinner parties. This recipe was quite fancy in its time and always a hit with guests.

INGREDIENTS
- 500 gm potatoes
- 2 tablespoons butter
- 1 cup milk
- 1 cup grated tasty cheese
- 3 tablespoons plain flour
- 1 teaspoon salt
- pepper

METHOD
1. Preheat oven to 160 degrees C or 350 degrees F.
2. Grease an ovenproof casserole dish.
3. Peel potatoes and cut into thick slices.
4. Put flour, salt, pepper and potatoes into a large plastic zipped bag.
5. Shake well until potatoes are well covered.
6. Place flour covered potatoes into the casserole dish.
7. Put milk and butter into a small saucepan and place saucepan on stove and heat over low heat until butter is melted.
8. Pour milk mixture over the potatoes.
9. Cover with grated cheese.
10. Cover the casserole, and bake in the oven for ¾ of an hour.
11. Take the lid off and cook for a further 15 minutes to allow the top layer to brown.

Stuffed Mushrooms

This can be used as an appetiser or an accompaniment to a main meal, but it's also filling enough to be enjoyed as a meal on it's own.

INGREDIENTS
- 250gm (½ lb) small mushrooms
- 1 small clove garlic (crushed)
- 1 dessertspoon chopped parsley
- 2 tablespoons soft breadcrumbs
- 2 oz butter
- Salt and pepper
- 3 shallots
- 1 tablespoon olive oil

METHOD
1. Preheat oven to 160 degrees Celcius or 350 degrees Farenheit.
2. Wash and stem mushrooms; chop stems finely.
3. Melt butter in frying pan, add mushroom stems and garlic, sauté for two minutes.
4. Add salt and pepper to taste, parsley and chopped shallots; cook gently for one minute.
5. Remove from heat and add enough breadcrumbs to mix to a light stuffing.
6. Fill mushroom caps with this mixture.
7. Place in a shallow well greased oven proof dish.
8. Bake in a moderate oven 10 – 15 minutes. Do not over cook.

Baked Tomato

Can be served as a starter, an accompaniment to a main meal or part of a vegetarian meal. Tomatoes give your main meal an edge with their tangy, sweet taste and colour.

INGREDIENTS
- 3 medium to large red ripe but firm vine tomatoes
- 1 cup chopped fresh chives
- 6 slices of tasty cheese
- salt and pepper to taste

METHOD
1. Preheat oven to 160 degrees Celcius or 350 degrees Farenheit.
2. Cut each tomato in half using the 'van dyke' method (which means to take your knife in and out around the centre of the tomato in a zig zag action)*see photograph on opposite page.
3. Season each tomato half with salt and pepper, put a few chives on top of each tomato (saving half for topping).
4. Place a slice of cheese on top and then sprinkle with remaining chives.
5. Bake in the oven for 10 to 15 minutes, or until cheese has melted and is golden.

Baked Carrots

Another 'fancy' recipe from the 1970s era of dinner parties and experimenting with French cooking - sweetening carrots was always a great success.

INGREDIENTS
- ¼ cup boiling salt water
- ¼ cup brown sugar
- ½ teaspoon grated lemon rind
- 2 tablespoons lemon juice
- ½ cup honey
- 1 teaspoon allspice
- 2 tablespoons butter

METHOD
1. Preheat oven to 180 degrees c or 350 degrees F.
2. Grease an oven proof casserole dish.
3. Place carrots and water in a saucepan, cover and simmer until tender.
4. Drain and reserve water.
5. Arrange the carrots in the casserole dish.
6. Mix the reserved water with all the remaining ingredients, EXCEPT THE BUTTER, and pour over the carrots.
7. Dot with the butter and bake in the oven for 20 minutes.

*Serves 6.

Parsnip Croquettes

The sweet flavour of the parsnip comes out with this dish. This is one of my favourites. I can never stop at one. A tasty treat on their own or an accompaniment with a main meal.

INGREDIENTS
- 1 lb parsnips
- 1 oz butter
- 1 small egg
- 2 rashers bacon
- Salt and pepper
- Extra egg for glazing
- Oil for frying
- ¾ cup milk
- 2 0r 3 tablespoons finely chopped chives or shallots
- 2 tablespoons plain flour
- Extra seasoned flour
- Dried breadcrumbs

METHOD
1. Remove rind from bacon and cut bacon into small pieces, fry until crisp, drain, set aside.
2. Peel parsnips, cut into small pieces; put parsnip into a saucepan with the milk, simmer covered until parsnips are tender and liquid is almost absorbed.
3. Remove from heat, add butter, chopped shallots, egg, plain flour and bacon.
4. Season with salt and pepper, mix well.
5. Drop spoonfuls of mixture into seasoned flour, shape into croquettes, roll in flour, dip in beaten egg, toss in dry breadcrumbs.
6. Press crumbs in firmly.
7. Refrigerate for one hour.
8. Deep fry in hot oil until golden brown.

*Makes approximately 18.

Baked Avocado

Baked Avocados make a nice side dish or a tasty breakfast or lunch meal - and for a vegetarian choice, simply omit the ham.

INGREDIENTS
- 2 Avocados
- 1 large clove garlic peeled and crushed
- 1 tablespoon finely chopped fresh chives
- 1 tablespoon finely chopped fresh parsley
- 3 slices of ham, finely chopped*
- Juice from 1 lemon
- Parmesan cheese, grated
- Cayenne pepper

METHOD
1. Preheat oven to 160 degrees C or 350 degrees F.
2. Cut avocados in half and remove stones.
3. Scoop out the flesh from the avocados, (carefully so as not to break the skin) and place the flesh into a bowl.
4. Add the garlic, chives, parsley and ham.
5. Mash them together and add the lemon juice for flavour and to stop the avocados browning.
6. Fill the avocado shells with the mixture.
7. Top each avocado with grated parmesan cheese and sprinkle of cayenne pepper.
8. Place the avocados into an oven proof dish and place in the oven.
9. Cook for 10-12 minutes.

Cauliflower au Gratin

Over the years we've definitely discovered that putting cheese on anything made it a great success with kids. Experimenting with Italian and French cooking opened up a whole world of adding amazing flavour to vegetables.

INGREDIENTS
- ½ small cauliflower
- 1 onion, peeled and chopped
- 30g (1 oz) butter
- 2 tablespoons plain flour
- 1 ½ cups milk
- ½ cup cream
- Salt and pepper
- 1 cup fresh breadcrumbs
- 60g (2 oz) grated tasty cheese

METHOD
1. Preheat oven to 180 degrees C or 350 degrees F.
2. Break cauliflower into flowerets, boil or steam until just tender.
3. Take off the heat and drain.
4. Place the cauliflower in an ovenproof dish.
5. Melt butter in a pan and add the onion. Cook stirring, until onion is transparent.
6. Add onion to the dish.
7. Reserve the butter in the pan.
8. Sift the flour into the reserved butter, cook over low heat, stirring for one minute.
9. Gradually stir in the milk and cream, stir until the sauce boils and thickens, season with salt and pepper, pour the sauce into the dish over the cauliflower and onion.
10. Stir to distribute sauce through cauliflower.
11. Sprinkle top evenly with combined breadcrumbs and cheese, baked uncovered in moderate oven for 20 minutes or until golden brown.

Buttered Cucumbers

People consider cucumbers to be a raw 'salad' vegetable and it is unusual to see them cooked these days. This is a delicious way to eat them though, and was popular during those dinner party days! This dish is especially delicious with fish.

INGREDIENTS
- 2 to 3 cucumbers
- 2 tablespoons melted butter
- Lemon juice
- Boiling salted water
- Salt and pepper
- 2 tablespoons chopped parsley

METHOD
1. Peel cucumbers, score them with fork. Cut into quarters, lengthwise or into ½ inch slices.
2. Drop cucumber into the boiling water, simmer for 2 minutes, drain.
3. Melt butter in frying pan, add well drained cucumber, sprinkle with salt and pepper.
4. Cook turning once, until cucumbers are lightly golden, do not overcook.
5. Add a good squeeze of lemon juice, stir this lightly through cucumbers.
6. Sprinkle with parsley.

Desserts

Desserts are the longed for end of the meal. From simple desserts, to an impressive, decadent, dessert.
Creating desserts is fun and rewarding. Fresh fruity desserts are the perfect finish to a summer meal and pies, puddings and crumbles are so welcome in the cold months.

Apple Crumble

Mum used to make apple crumble for us because it made stewed fruit a little more interesting. There are a lot of versions of the 'crumble' - it often depended what was in the cupboard! Sometimes it was just the flour and sugar.

INGREDIENTS
- 3-4 large cooking apples
- ½ cup plain flour
- ¾ cup brown sugar
- 2 tablespoons coconut
- ½ teaspoon cinnamon
- 90 g (3 oz) butter

METHOD
1. Preheat oven to 180 degrees C or 350 degrees F.
2. Grease an ovenproof dish. Peel, core and slice apples, place in the ovenproof dish.
3. Combine flour, sugar, coconut and cinnamon in a mixing bowl, rub in butter until mixture resembles fine breadcrumbs.
4. Sprinkle crumble mixture evenly over apples, bake in a moderate oven for 30-40 minutes or until apples are tender.

*Serves 4

*This crumble topping can be put on other fruit for example pear, peach, apricot, rhubarb or what ever fruit is in season.
You can also combine fruit (eg. apple and rhubarb).

Lemon Meringue Pie

This is one of my mum and my husband's favourite dessert. I remember being taught to make a version of this at school and I absolutely love the meringue on the top.

INGREDIENTS
- 1 quantity of Sweet Short Crust Pastry (pg 19)

Lemon Filling:
- 2 tablespoons cornflour
- ½ cup castor sugar
- 150ml (1/4 pint) water
- 1 lemon
- 1 ½ egg-yolks

Meringue:
- 2 egg-whites
- ½ cup castor sugar

METHOD
1. Preheat oven to 200 degrees C or 400 degrees F.
2. Roll out the chilled dough on to a lightly floured surface in a circle large enough to line the flan tin.
3. Line the tin with pastry and trim edges.
4. Prick base with a fork, place greaseproof paper over the pastry and sprinkle with a layer of dried beans or rice.
5. Bake in the oven for 10 minutes, remove paper and beans or rice and return to oven for further 3 minutes.
6. Remove from the oven and set aside while preparing the filling.
7. Place corn flour and castor sugar in a small saucepan.
8. Stir in water gradually and mix well to blend.
9. Finely grate the rind off the lemon.
10. Add the finely grated lemon rind into the mixture and cook over moderate heat, stirring all the time until thickened and boiling.
11. Remove the pan from heat and add the beaten egg-yolks and lemon juice.
12. Pour mixture into baked pie shell.
13. Beat egg whites until stiff, add half the sugar and beat, then add the other half of the sugar and beat again.
14. Spoon meringue over the filling, taking care to bring meringue to edge of the pastry.
15. Return to oven and cook for 10-12 minutes until golden brown.

Chocolate Mousse

This dessert appeared in the 1970's in restaurants and is still popular today. This is the recipe myself and my friend's made when we were entertaining.

INGREDIENTS
- 220 g (7 oz) dark eating chocolate, chopped *
- 4 eggs, separated
- ½ cup castor sugar
- 300ml (10 fliud oz or ½ pint) cream
- Extra whipped cream and chocolate curls to decorate (optional)

*A light milk chocolate can also be used.

METHOD
1. Place chocolate in a heatproof bowl.
2. Sit bowl over a pan of simmering water.
3. Stir until chocolate is almost melted.
4. Continue to stir until chocolate is smooth.
5. Remove from heat, cool slightly and gradually add the egg yolks until well blended and mixture is smooth, thick and glossy**
6. Whip cream. DO NOT OVER WHIP OR THE CREAM WILL BE DIFFICULT TO FOLD IN; cream should be just nicely thickened.
7. Fold the cream into the chocolate mixture.
8. Beat egg whites until soft peaks form. Again DO NOT OVER BEAT the whites or they will not fold easily into the chocolate mixture.
9. Fold in half the egg whites gently, then fold in the other half until well combined.
10 Spoon the mousse mixture in 6 small bowls or glasses (1 cup capacity).
11. Refrigerate, covered, for several hours or overnight.
12. Decorate as desired and serve.

** ** 1 tablespoon brandy can be added in here if desired.

Jam Roly Poly

When I was growing up as a child we always had sweets after the main evening meal (a tradition I followed with my children). when the cupboards when getting low in supplies this was a good standby. We all had a turn at picking which flavour of jam to go in the rolly.

INGREDIENTS
- 2 cups plain flour
- 125gm (4oz) butter
- 1 teaspoon baking powder
- Pinch salt
- 4 tablespoons water
- A squeeze lemon juice
- Jam -flavour of your choice
- Milk for glazing

METHOD
1. Preheat oven to 200 degrees C or 400 degrees F.
2. Grease an oven tray.
3. Sift dry ingredients into a bowl.
4. Rub in the butter with your fingertips until it resembles dry breadcrumbs.
5. Add the water and the lemon juice and using a fork mix to a pliable dough.
6. Turn dough onto a lightly floured board, knead lightly.
7. Roll the pastry out to a rectangle shape.
8. Moisten the rectangle edges with milk.
9. Spread the centre part with jam.
10. Roll up, pressing the edges well together.
11. Place on the greased oven tray.
12. Bake in the oven for 15 to 20 minutes.

*Serve with custard.

Treacle Pudding

This dish was popular when I was a child. Mum use to make it the winter months when fresh fruit was scarce and the supplies were getting low, it was cheap to make and filling and warm on a cold winter's night.

INGREDIENTS
- 90gm (3oz) butter
- 90gm (3oz) sugar
- 180gm (6oz)S.R. Flour
- 2 teaspoons ground ginger
- 1 large egg (beaten with a fork)
- 4 tablespoons milk
- 1 teaspoon vanilla essence
- 1 ½ tablespoons golden syrup

METHOD
1. Lightly grease a heatproof basin or steamer pudding bowl, also grease some greaseproof paper to go over your bowl if you do not have a pudding steamer with a lid.
2. Put water into a large pot that is big enough to hold your pudding steamer or basin, and that has enough water to come up over half to two thirds of the basin. Put the pot onto your hotplate with lid on, turn on to boil, whilst making your pudding.
3. Sift flour and ginger.
4. Cream butter and sugar, add beaten gradually, then add flour mixture and milk alternately.
5. Add vanilla essence and mix well.
6 Put golden syrup into the bottom of the basin, or pudding steamer, then add the pudding mixture on top.
7. Cover with pudding steamer lid or greased paper that is then secured with string around the rim of the basin.
8. Carefully lower the basin or pudding steamer into the large pot of boiling water.
9. Put the lid on the large pot.
10. Turn heat to low and steam for 1 ½ hour.
11. DO NOT LET THE WATER RUN DRY, CHECK ALL THE TIME AND TOP WITH BOILING WATER WHEN NEEDED.

*Serve with custard, cream or ice cream.

*Instead of ginger and golden syrup, you can also use: 2 tbsp jam OR 2 tbsp cocoa OR 120gm (4oz) stoned, chopped dates.

Chocolate Pudding

When I was a kid, family used to cook chocolate steam pudding and then a separate sauce. In the late 1960s, I remember being given a recipe for a self saucing pudding...just as tasty and so much easier!

INGREDIENTS
- 60gm (2oz) butter
- ½ cup sugar
- 1 egg
- 1 cup self-raising flour
- 2 dessertspoons cocoa
- ½ teaspoon vanilla essence
- Extra ½ cup sugar
- Extra 2 dessertspoons cocoa
- 1 ½ cups hot water

METHOD
1. Preheat oven to 180 degrees C or 350 degrees F.
2. Grease an ovenproof dish.
3. Place butter and sugar in a bowl and cream until light and fluffy.
4. Add egg and vanilla essence and beat well.
5. Fold in sifted flour and cocoa alternately with the milk.
6. Place the mixture into the greased dish.
7. Mix the extra sugar and cocoa together and sprinkle over the mixture.
8. Finally pour the hot water over the top very gently.
9. Bake in the oven for 35 to 40 minutes.

Golden Syrup Dumplings

My mum enjoyed these as a child, so it's a recipe that has lasted the test of time. They were very popular around the Depression and World War II at a time when treats were scarce and simple ingredients were used to cook with.

INGREDIENTS
Dumplings:
- 1 cup S.R. Flour
Pinch of salt
- 1 tablespoon butter
- 1 egg (lightly beaten)
- Sufficient mik to make a stiff dough

Syrup:
- 2 cups boiling water
- ½ cup sugar
- 1 tablespoon butter
- 1 tablespoon golden syrup

METHOD
1. Sift flour and salt in to a bowl.
2. Rub in the butter and add the egg and sufficient milk to make a stiff dough.
3. In a large saucepan put the sugar, butter and golden syrup, add the boiling water and stir until dissolved over medium heat on a hotplate on your stove.
4. Drop dessertspoonfuls into the syrup, after five minutes turn the dumplings over, reduce heat and cook for another 15 -20 minutes.

*Serve with custard, or cream.

Apple Pie

My granny used to make a beautiful apple pie - apples always seemed to be a staple in all homes and many people had an apple tree in their backyard. Apples, combined with an inexpensive pastry, meant an easy and tasty dessert.

INGREDIENTS
- 1 quantity of 250 gm (8oz) sweet short pastry (page 19)
- 4 large cooking apples
- 1 teaspoon lemon juice
- ¼ cup castor sugar
- ½ teaspoon nutmeg
- 2 cloves
- Egg white for glazing
- Extra castor sugar for glazing

METHOD
1. Preheat oven to 220 degrees C or 425 degrees F.
2. Peel, quarter and ore apples; cut into slices.
3. Place apples into a saucepan with the water, gloves and lemon juice and cook until barely tender.
4. Remove cloves, add sugar and nutmeg: cool.
5. Take pastry out of the refrigerator and cut off two-thirds of the pastry.
6. Roll out the pastry to line a 23cm (9inch) pie plate, making sure you take the pastry up the sides of the pie plate.
7. Fill with the cooked apple, brush the edges of the pastry with water.
8. Roll remaining pastry to cover the apples.
9. Press edges and trim.
10. Brush the top with egg-white, sprinkle with castor sugar.
11. Bake 10 minutes in a hot oven, then reduce heat to moderate 180 degrees C or 350 degrees F, and bake for a further 20 minutes.

Pavlova Roll

This dessert is fresh and light, a perfect after dinner treat and a lot easier to make than you think.

INGREDIENTS
- 4 egg whites
- a pinch of salt
- ¾ cup (115g/4 oz) caster sugar
- 1 teaspoon cornflour
- 1 ½ teaspoons white vinegar
- ½ teaspoon vanilla essence
- Extra caster sugar for dusting

Filling:
- 1 ¼ cups (300 ml /10 ½ fl oz) cream
- 1 tablespoon icing sugar
- ½ teaspoon vanilla essence
- ¾ cup fresh strawberries, hulled and diced

(Beat cream together with icing sugar and vanilla essence until thick.)

METHOD
1. Preheat oven to 160 degrees C/350 degrees F.
2. Grease and line a 26cm x 30cm (11 inch x 12 inch) Swiss roll tin with baking paper (cut the paper slightly larger than the tin so it overhangs and stands up a little all the way around.
3. Whip the egg white with a pinch of salt until stiff peaks form.
4. Add the caster sugar 2 tablespoons at a time until the mixture is stiff, fluffy and glossy and the sugar is dissolved.
5. Fold through the vanilla, cornflour and vinegar.
6. Spread mixture evenly into the tin and bake for 10-15 minutes until set and very slightly coloured.
7. Whilst pavlova is baking. Place a large sheet of baking paper on your bench and sprinkle caster sugar lightly and evenly over the baking paper.
8. Gently invert pavlova onto the prepared paper, then gently peel away the lining paper. Leave to cool then top with whipped cream and cut berries.
9. Roll up with the paper from the long side, place the roll onto a serving plate, seam side down.
10. Slide and push the roll with a spatula towards the end of the paper so you can easily pull the paper out.
11. Cover the finished roll with cream and garnish with strawberries.

To serve, cut into thick slices.
Serves 8

Brandy Snaps

This is handy when you don't have anything fresh in the cupboard and you need to impress a last minute guest! Cream is the only fresh item that you need. When my children were young, we didn't live close to a store, so recipes like these were very welcome.

INGREDIENTS
- 1 cup flour
- 2 teaspoons ground ginger
- 1/3 cup golden syrup or treacle
- ½ cup castor sugar
- ½ cup butter
- 2 teaspoons water
- Whipped cream

METHOD
1. Pre heat oven to 180 degrees C or 350 degrees F.
2. Grease 2 baking trays.
3. Sift together flour and ginger in a bowl and rub in the butter.
4. Place the golden syrup or treacle, water and sugar in a saucepan and warm over low heat.
5. Make a well in the centre of the flour and add liquid mixture from the saucepan.
6. Stir until thoroughly mixed.
7. On a greased tray place walnut size pieces of the mixture (allow room for mixture to spread whilst baking).
8. Bake in the oven for 10-12 minutes or until golden brown.
9. Remove from oven and roll quickly around the handle of a greased wooden spoon.
10. When cold fill with whipped cream.

Cream Puffs

These are delicious savoury or sweet. We've filled them with cream but they are great with chicken, asparagus and white sauce for a lovely savoury version or cover them in chocolate sauce to create a mini chocolate éclair!

INGREDIENTS
- 1 heaped tablespoon butter
- ½ cup boiling water
- ½ cup sifted S.R. flour
- 2 eggs

METHOD
1. Preheat oven 180 degrees C or 350 degrees F.
2. Grease an oven tray.
3. Melt the butter in a saucepan, then add the boiling water.
4. Return to heat.
5. When the mixture boils up add the S.R. flour and mix quickly.
6. Remove from heat and add eggs one at a time, and beat until the mixture is smooth and glossy.
7. Place dessertspoonfuls of mixture, onto the greased tray.
8. Bake in the oven for 25-30 minutes.
9. Make a small incision in each cream puff to allow the steam to escape and the centre dry out.
10. Cool, then fill puffs with whipped cream or a custard filling.

*Usually when making Choux Pastry you use Plain flour where as in this recipe you use Self Raising flour. I have been using this recipe for forty years now and I refer to these as my 'never fail cream puffs' - you can't go wrong!

Rhubarb Sponge

Rhubarb is an easy plant to grow in your garden. It is classed as a vegetable but the tender pink shoots are treated as fruit. When rhubarb is combined with apple it makes a delicious dessert.

INGREDIENTS
- 5 cups (425 g /15oz) chopped rhubarb
- 2 medium apples, peeled, cored and thinly sliced
- ¼ cup (55g/2oz) caster sugar
- 1 teaspoon grated lemon rind
- ¼ cup (60ml/2 fl oz) water
- 2 eggs
- 1/3 cup (70g/2 ½ oz) extra caster sugar
- 2 tablespoons cornflour
- 2 tablespoons plain flour
- 2 tablespoon self raising flour
- 1 tablespoons custard powder

METHOD
1. Preheat oven to 180 degrees C/350 degrees F.
2. Grease the inside of a deep (6 cup capacity /1.5 litre /2 ½ pints) ovenproof dish.
3. Combine rhubarb, apples, sugar, lemon rind and water in a saucepan, bring to boil, reduce heat, simmer, covered for about 15 minutes or until the rhubarb and apple are tender.
4. Pour hot rhubarb/apple mixture into the greased dish.
5. Beat eggs in a bowl with an electric mixer, until thick and creamy, gradually add extra sugar, beat until dissolved between each addition.
6. Sift flours and custard powder over egg mixture, and fold thoroughly.
7. Spread mixture evenly over hot rhubarb/apple mixture.
8. Bake for about 30 minutes, or until sponge is cooked when tested with a skewer.

Serve with ice-cream.
Serves 4-6 people.

Lemon Cheesecake

Philadelphia cheese was used for just about everything in the 1970s and cheesecakes quickly became a popular dessert because of this. This is delicious plain - we just used some lemon rind on top - but you can go all out with cream, chocolate swirls and more.

INGREDIENTS
- 250 g (8 oz) finely crushed, sweet biscuits
- 125g (4 oz) butter, melted
- ¼ teaspoon cinnamon
- ¼ teaspoon nutmeg
- 250 g (8 oz) packet of cream cheese, softened
- 300ml (10 fl oz or ½ pt) sour cream
- 1 cup castor sugar
- 2 x 59g (2 oz) eggs
- Grated rind of 1 lemon
- ¼ cup lemon juice
- 1 teaspoon vanilla extract

METHOD
1. Preheat oven to 170 degrees C or 325 degrees F.
2. Combine biscuit crumbs, cinnamon, nutmeg and melted butter together.
3. Press mixture firmly into the base and up the sides of a 22cm (8 inch) spring-form pan.
4. Refrigerate for 15 minutes.
5. In a mixing bowl beat the cream cheese, sour cream, sugar, lemon rind and vanilla essence until smooth, add the lemon juice, then beat in eggs one at a time.
6. Pour mixture into the chilled crumb crust then bake in the preheated oven for about 30 minutes.
7. Turn off the oven and allow the cheesecake to cool in the oven.
8. Refrigerate cheesecake for several hours or overnight.
9. Remove cheesecake from spring-form pan and transfer to a serving plate.
10. Sieve top lightly with cinnamon or nutmeg and scatter some lemon rind on top.
11. Cut into wedges and serve.

Dieting

Life was definitely different a few generations ago.

Without computers, iPods, mobile phones and two cars per family everyone rode a bike, walked and played outside.

They spent time in the garden, mowing lawns, weeding and doing more physical chores. Washing clothes and dishes now happen with the push of a button but, not so long ago, took a lot of physical exertion.

Likewise, preparing food took time and energy – it wasn't quick. A refrigerator and mix master only became available in 1955.

They did not have fast food options. You made your own jam, sauce and pickles and bottled fruit and vegetables when it was plentiful so it could be used out of season.

You only cooked what you needed and there weren't options for dinner or sweets. What was made was all there was – eat or go hungry.

Everything was home made. Chocolate and lollies were a luxury for special occasions.

Fast food, crisps and having restaurant meals were unheard of. Going out for breakfast, lunch or even a 'cuppa' just didn't happen for the average person, and it certainly didn't happen on a regular basis.

In saying all of that, people still worried about their weight. My mother often told me about the foolish (and often dangerous) diets that her and her peers would indulge in for the sake of a few kilos.

Today, there is the popularity of Paleo and LCHF, but that's simply Atkins from the late 80s/early 90s repackaged. The Cabbage Soup Diet was also popular in the 80s, and in the 70s it was the Israeli Army Diet, in the 60s it was all about the liquid lunch, and in the 50s it was the awful Tapeworm Diet (yes, that's just what it sounds like). In the 30s it was the Grapefruit Diet and in the 20s it was cigarettes and coffee. In fact, recorded crazy diets go back as far as the 1720s where writer, Thomas Short, encouraged people to move away from swamps in order to lose weight!

In the 1970s, the biggest chance to our diet was artifical sweeteners providing a seemingly guilt-free sugar addiction, and the introduction of the healthy diet pyramid that discouraged fats and promoted grains. The backlash against carbohydrates in the 90s has meant that an entire generation of people are completely and utterly confused about what 'healthy' truly means.

I think that perhaps my grandparents had it right, purely because they had no other choice.

Eat simply.

Eat what is in season and what is easily accessible.

Ensure that fresh vegetables are a large part of each meal.

Steer clear of preservatives (anything that isn't in a tin and survives for months on end in the cupboard can't possibly be healthy).

Don't deprive yourself of a sweet treat, but take your time making it and share it with loved ones to ensure you are consuming in moderation!

Food should be enjoyable, and it definitely shouldn't take over your life.

Making Memories

There is nothing more special than a handwritten recipe. My mother, my aunts and my grandmother all generously handed down their cooking favourites and it's such an honour to be able to share them with my loved ones, and to remember them each time I cook. Use the pages overleaf to keep a record of yours.

Pumpkin Scones
6oz butter ¼ cup caster sugar
½ cup cooked mashed pumpkin
1 egg beaten ½ teas salt
½ cup of milk 2½ cups SR flour

cream butter & sugar until light
Stir in pumpkin & egg
sift flour & salt & stir in
Mix to soft dough with milk
Pat or roll to 2cm thick
shape, place scones on a
greased tin. Leaving red oven
at 220°C brush with milk & bake 15 mins

Ginger biscuits
¼ lb marg.   1 cup sugar
1   egg   2 tbsp golden syrup
2 cups SR flour   2 teas ground ginger

cream sugar & marg. add egg & gol syrup
mix well sift flour & ginger & add to
mixture. Place in teas. on greased slide
and bake in a fairly hot oven 425°?

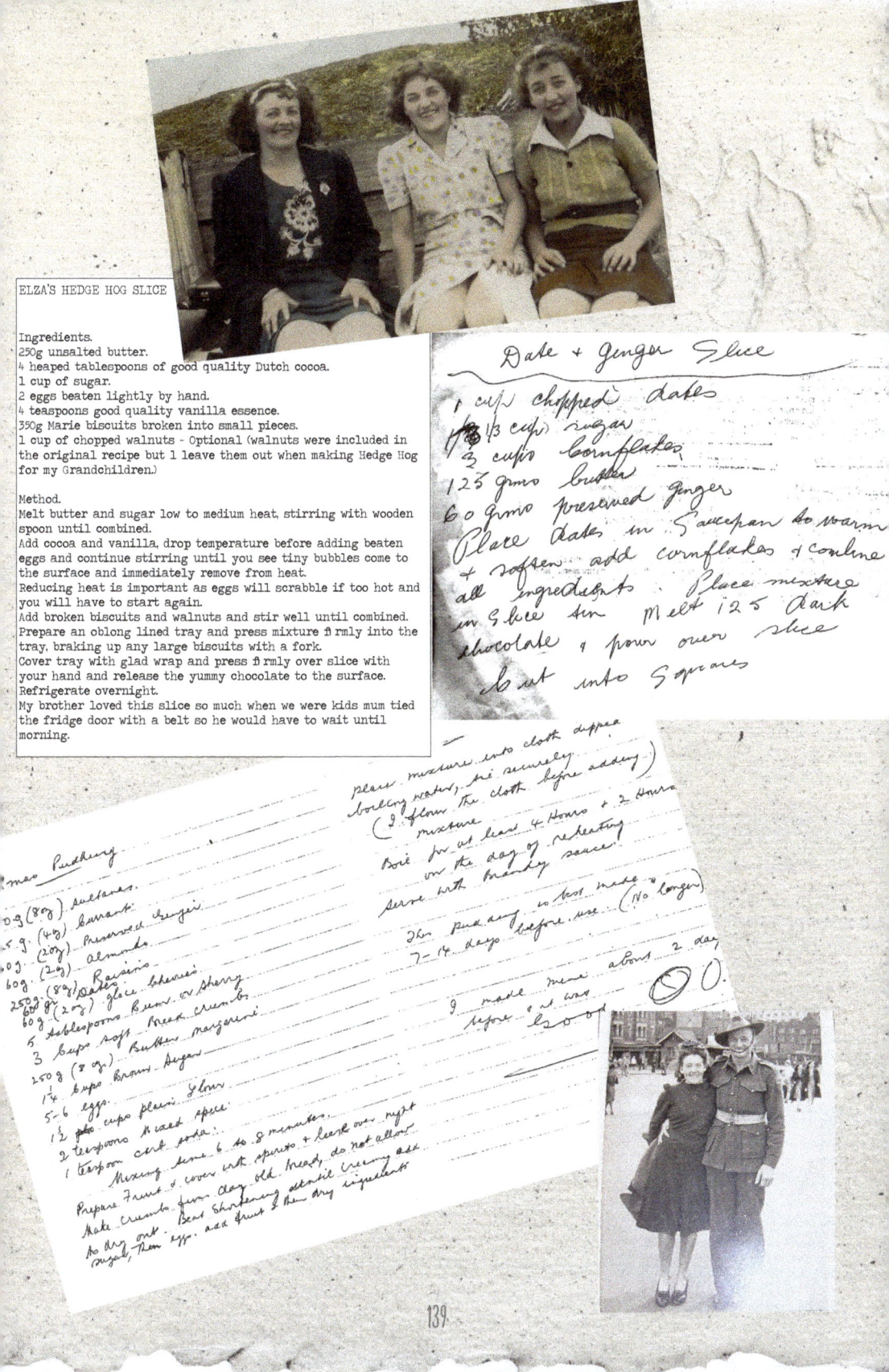

ELZA'S HEDGE HOG SLICE

Ingredients.
250g unsalted butter.
4 heaped tablespoons of good quality Dutch cocoa.
1 cup of sugar.
2 eggs beaten lightly by hand.
4 teaspoons good quality vanilla essence.
350g Marie biscuits broken into small pieces.
1 cup of chopped walnuts - Optional (walnuts were included in the original recipe but I leave them out when making Hedge Hog for my Grandchildren.)

Method.
Melt butter and sugar low to medium heat, stirring with wooden spoon until combined.
Add cocoa and vanilla, drop temperature before adding beaten eggs and continue stirring until you see tiny bubbles come to the surface and immediately remove from heat.
Reducing heat is important as eggs will scrabble if too hot and you will have to start again.
Add broken biscuits and walnuts and stir well until combined.
Prepare an oblong lined tray and press mixture firmly into the tray, braking up any large biscuits with a fork.
Cover tray with glad wrap and press firmly over slice with your hand and release the yummy chocolate to the surface.
Refrigerate overnight.
My brother loved this slice so much when we were kids mum tied the fridge door with a belt so he would have to wait until morning.

Date & Ginger Slice

1 cup chopped dates
1/3 cup sugar
3 cups cornflakes
125 gms butter
60 gms preserved ginger

Place dates in saucepan to warm & soften, add cornflakes & combine all ingredients. Place mixture in slice tin. Melt 125 dark chocolate & pour over slice. Cut into squares.

Xmas Pudding

250g (8oz) sultanas
125g (4oz) currants
60g (2oz) preserved ginger
60g (2oz) almonds
250g (8oz) raisins
60g (2oz) glacé cherries
⅓ cup Rum or sherry
3 tablespoons soft bread crumbs
250g (8oz) Butter margarine
1¼ cups brown sugar
5-6 eggs
1½ cups plain flour
2 teaspoons mixed spice
1 teaspoon carb soda

Mixing time 6 to 8 minutes.
Prepare Fruit & cover with spirits & leave over night.
Make crumbs from day old bread, do not allow to dry out. Beat shortening until creamy add sugar, then eggs. Add fruit & then dry ingredients place mixture into cloth dipped in boiling water, tie securely. (I flour the cloth before adding mixture)
Boil for at least 4 hours + 2 hours on the day of reheating
Serve with brandy sauce.

This pudding is best made (No longer) 7-14 days before use.
I made mine about 2 days before & it was good.

Index

Aioli 45
Apple Crumble 111
Apples, Rhubarb Apple Sponge 133
Apple Pie 125
Apple Sauce 71
Avocado, Baked Avocado 103
Bacon, Bacon Scone Roll 35
Bacon, Egg & Bacon Pie 67
Baked Avocado 103
Baked Carrots 99
Baked Cucumbers 107
Baked Lamb Chops 89
Baked Stuffed Topside 75
Baked Tomato 97
Beef, Baked Stuffed Topside 75
Beef Burgundy 79
Beef, Carpet Bag Steak 77
Beef, Silverside 73
Beef, Steak & Kidney Pie 63
Brandy Snaps 129
Bubble & Squeak 37
Butter, Garlic 23
Butter, Herb 21
Carrots, Baked Carrots 99
Cauliflower au Gratin 105
Carpet Bag Steak 77
Cheese & Tomato Flan 69
Chicken, Chicken Broth 31
Chicken, Farmers Chicken Casserole 87
Chicken Mushroom Pie 65
Chocolate Mousse 115
Chocolate Pudding 121
Cold Meat Fritters 39
Cornish Pasty 61
Cream Puffs 131
Cucumbers, Baked Cucumbers 107
Egg & Bacon Pie 67
Farmers Chicken Casserole 87
Garlic Butter 23
Golden Syrup Dumplings 123
Ham, Pea & Ham Soup 27
Herb Butter 21
Herbed Rack of Lamb 81
Jam Roly Poly 117
Lamb, Baked Lamb Chops 89
Lamb, Herbed Rack of Lamb 81
Lamb, Lamb & Vege Soup 29
Lemon Cheesecake 135
Lemon Meringue Pie 113
Mayonnaise 43

Mushroom, Chicken Mushroom Pie 65
Mushroom Sauce 51
Mushrooms, Stuffed Mushrooms 95
Mustard Sauce 55
Parsnip Croquettes 101
Pastry, Short Crust Pastry 18
Pastry, Sweet Short Crust Pastry 19
Pavlova Roll 127
Peas, Pea & Ham Soup 27
Pepper Sauce 53
Pork, Roast Pork 71
Potatoes, Scalloped Potatoes 93
Red Wine Sauce 57
Rhubarb Apple Sponge 133
Roast Pork 71
Sauce, Aioli 45
Sauce, Apple 71
Sauce, Mayonnaise 43
Sauce, Mushroom 51
Sauce, Mustard 55
Sauce, Pepper 53
Sauce, Red Wine 57
Sauce, Seafood 49
Sauce, Tartare 47
Scalloped Potatoes 93
Scones, Savoury Scones 33
Seafood Sauce 49
Short Crust Pastry 18
Silverside 73
Steak & Kidney Pie 63
Stuffed Mushrooms 95
Sweet Short Crust Pastry 19
Tartare Sauce 47
Tomato, Baked Tomato 97
Tomato, Cheese & Tomato Flan 69
Treacle Pudding 119
Tuna Rice Slice 85
Veal Cordon Bleu 83
Vegetables, Bubble & Squeak 37
Vegetables, Lamb & Vege Soup 29
Vegetables, Cornish Pasty 61

www.ingramcontent.com/pod-product-compliance
Lightning Source LLC
Chambersburg PA
CBHW040510110526
44587CB00045B/4200